21 HUSTLES
AND SMALL BUSINESSES
FOR THE YOUTH

Youth Entrepreneurship

Phil Lewis

Publisher: Phil Lewis Publishing, LLC
Editor: Jordan Hughes
Cover Designer: Jordan Hughes

Paperback ISBN: 978-1-7357876-0-2
eBook ISBN: 978-1-7357876-1-9

PRINTED IN THE UNITED STATES OF AMERICA

Dedication

This book is dedicated to all of my friends who grinded with me in my early years. My Brother John aka "Country Boy" Who hook me up with the hustle. Cheyanne aka " Sky Rolla" Joseph aka "Fat Rat" Anthony aka " jail bird" Hustlin' on Crenshaw to Compton every day or just on the weekends, we made it happen. Rain or hot weather we pushed through it. I hope I did not leave anyone out if I did forgive me. This is the early years..

Table of Contents

INTRODUCTION

Many of you don't have much money in your pocket... No clothes or food in your fridge. It probably seems as if no one loves you or cares about you, but I'm here to tell you that God loves you and he has your back as long as you believe in Him. You can also make it out of your stressful conditions, and it will come to pass if you do what's right and stay out of trouble. It's unbelievable how people expect you to do well in school when you have gone without food and clean clothes, and no haircut in months along with being surrounded by drugs or bad influences. Then when you return home you don't always have a mother or father to greet you, and you have to sleep on the floor accompanied by five other people with rats and roaches racing on the floor. This is the life that some of my homies lived in there upbringing. So then you get tired and fed up and want to improve your living conditions. Restaurants and stores deny your job application constantly despite of jobs being available. Same scenario over and over again. If you're still broke and in need of money, this book is for you. For those of you that don't have an uncle to put you on game, please allow Uncle Phil to lace you with some game. It's time, young people, to get up and go get that money. Let's go!

MY STORY
IN SHORTFORM...

My name is Phillip Johnson. I grew up with 7 brothers and 4 sisters in the same household making a total of 12. There was always someone moving in and out. My father was a pastor and my mother was the first lady of our little family church. My parents did the best they could, but sometimes things got out of control. My parents separated often, and when this happens usually the younger kids stay with mom while the older with the dad. But I love my parents, R.I.P. to my father. My side hustle began when I was about 9 years old. My brother John and I would collect cans or help our aunties and uncles for money. I also started cutting grass, washing cars, and cleaning back yards... whatever I could to make money. Because it was so many of us, I could not always get the new pair of Jordan's or 3-piece chicken combos I wanted from my parents. I even wanted bikes and mopeds. One day when I was about 14 my brother John came home with $25 dollars. He said that he got a job with a man named Bro Matt selling music and car freshener. So, I pleaded with my brother to get me a job with this man, and he promised to hook me up. To be honest, he was not a raw hustler like myself. Not being able to sleep at night I thought to myself... if he could make $25 then I can make $50. Bro. Matt sold music and items around the corner at the car wash. After my mother met him, my brother and I began to work around the corner at the car wash and sell music to those customers. Bro. Matt would come around 6 pm and pay us for the items we sold that day. Man, this changed my life. After knowing Bro. Matt for a while, he asked if we wanted to go sell on Crenshaw which was on the Westside of town. We both said yes. He would drop us off on Crenshaw & Stocker, and say, "I'll be back in 7 hours to meet you here". So we walked and sold. My brother did not like this new way of selling.

He preferred to sit up at the car washes. Continuing on, he didn't last in this hustle. As for me, I was in heaven! Boy I made about $175 in 5 hours. During this time, my father and mother got back together. My father started a room & board house with 9 bedrooms on the Westside 10 minutes from Crenshaw. We all moved back in. This is when things changed for the worse. My father began renting some of the rooms out to non-family; this resulted in some issues. The community was surrounded by gang members, dope selling, and prostitutes. Eventually, a few of my brothers began to sell drugs whether it be outside of the house or the on the porch. I remember seeing drugs addicts lined up as my brother served them. I also remember the police pulling everyone out of the house. I witnessed drive-bys right in front of me. Someone was always getting shot. I decided I didn't want that life.

Thank God I had a way to make legitimate money. The police would buy music from me all the time. When I turned

16, I was a beast. Brother Matt hired 5 more kids to join the group. I was number 1, nickname "Sharp Shooter". My strategy was that I would make sure that I looked my best. I would walk the Crenshaw strip for almost 10 hours hitting up barbershops, restaurants, clinics, banks, and gas stations. I would gross over $250 on a Saturday, my commission was about $100. Monday through Friday, after school, I would make about $40 a day. At the end of the week, I would have about $300. I purchased my first car for $600 from my brother Steve. My friends who sold drugs would ask me how can I purchase something so fresh. I told them that I sold music, car fresheners, hats, incense, and even umbrellas, if it was raining. I encouraged them to try my hustle opposed to their drug-selling method telling them that if you can sell drugs, you can sell anything. It's as simple as switching the product while keeping the same energy. Their first day of selling went well.

When I turned 17, I got tired of the laborious work. I decided to put in an application at all of the fast food places that were hiring nearby. I never got hired. One of my friends then told me that he was hired at McDonald's, but only made $120 a week, this is when I decided to continue my hustle. I not only made more than him, but I had freedom. I decided to go on my own with the selling, this way, all of the profit went to me. This was simple because I knew where to buy the best products and how to sell them effectively. On my first day of being my own boss, I made $400. I blew up fast and was making so much progress that I had people who wanted to work for me. I kept 40% of their profit and 10%

for reinvestment. At age 17, I was making an easy $800 a week.

I began to expand with different products. To start off, I had 6 friends selling under me. Two sold candy, two sold home-made cookies, and one sold car fresheners and incense, I had a few other people selling music under me. Every product was sold, but the cookies sold the fastest making them $100 in 3 hours. The incense crew sold 100 packs of incense and 65 car fresheners at $1 each making a total of $165.

There is nothing like earning money legally and righteously. There is no need to feel guilty about your work or worry if you will get caught doing something illegal. I will give you the knowledge on how these hustles can lead into a business. In this book I will describe the things I have done to earn money. First, I am going to touch on small businesses that can be started with no money. You only need the desire to succeed. You cannot be lazy and afraid. If you lack the mo-tivation, have a family member or friend join you on the start of this venture. Make sure whomever you choose isn't negative or irresponsible. Always remember you work hard now to play later. I'd like to share something that was very beneficial to me, it was the prayer I would say. It went some-thing like this:

Father God I'm grateful that you have given me the oppor-tunity to sell these things. I pray that you give me boldness and confidence to talk to people. I ask that you allow me to sell out today. Please watch over us and protects us in Jesus name. Amen.

This prayer helped me to be fearless and able to sell out when the effort was put forth.

Let's begin:

No money to start for Hustle #1- #14

HUSTLE #1

Back Yard Cleaning and Garage Clean Up

Requirements: Gloves, trash bags
(which you can get from the client) and maybe 1 friend

Many kids left home or simply don't want to do this work. Just be ready to do hands on work. Make 200 fliers and write something similar to "Young, strong, and ready to work students for backyard and garage clean up for very cheap. Number (123) 456-7891 Text or call." Now put on some clothes that look like you are able to get dirty and put on your gloves. Start on your block. Go to the door with your gloves on; this is your uniform. Knock on the door, and when they answer it, step back a few steps to give them space. Say:

Hello Ma'am or Sir. my name is ( ). I live around the corner. We are out today cleaning backyards and garages, and we are ready right now. Do you have work for us today? We are trying to earn money for school clothes.

Never lie about your reason. Be truthful. If your mother needs money for a light bill or you need money for food, just tell them. If they say no, leave them your flyer. You will get some work… trust me. If they ask how much for your service, tell them to be fair and ask what the work is worth to them. If the price sounds good, then go for it. Always be respectful. Never wear your pants down or sagging. Don't use foul language on their property. Address them as Sir or Ma'am, Always.

HUSTLE #2

Babysitting
(targeted toward young ladies)

This is simply one of the oldest forms of making money. We have all done it for free, so now let's get paid for. Exposure is key to this business. Of course, get your parent's permission before beginning. Start with your family & friends. Call your aunts, cousins, etc. Let them know that you can babysit for date nights, business outings, and any time needed. If you don't have a cell phone, give them your parents number. I do not recommend babysitting for strangers.

HUSTLE #3

Door to Door Car Washing

***Requirements: 1 bucket, dish washing soap, Shemmys
or a towel. These items are usually in your home.***

Before you start this venture, ask your parents, friends, or
neighbors to wash their cars for free. You want to learn how
to do a good job. If you don't know how to wash cars, ask an
adult to teach you. Remember to clean the windows thor-
oughly. When you are done, ask an adult evaluate the car.

Use the door to door strategy. Make sure that you have
about 200 flyers. It can read something like: "Students washing cars; door to door service from your friendly neighbors."
Make sure your number is listed. Go to the door with a bucket and soap. Put the Shemmy around your neck or shoulder.
This will give the appearance that you are ready to wash cars.
A good price is $10; you can also ask for a donation. Most
of the time they will give you way more than the $10. If you
come across an elderly person who is in need of a car wash,
and they genuinely don't have money, wash their car for free.
At least wash the windows. God will bless you.

HUSTLE #4

Help People Move

Requirements: Gloves

Put up an ad on Offer Up, Craigslist, and Facebook. Go and post up at a uhaul store.. You can advertise locally within 5 miles. Remember to post up your ad 3-4 times a day. You can ride a bike or walk to the job. The ad can go like: "Student(s) ready to work and help you move". Take a good picture of yourself or with your friends. That's if they want to earn work as well; I strongly encourage you to have someone to help. You will be surprised at how many people need help moving things.

HUSTLE #5

Passing Out Flyers For Businesses

Requirements: None

This one is one of my favorites. It's dear to my heart. Why? Because I have owned many restaurants (you can read it toward the end of the book). I would look for people to pass out my flyers to bring people in. Most fast food places are in a center or around large parking lots. They usually need someone to pass out coupons for the business. The strategy is to pass out flyers in an area where there are many people.

So, who needs this service? Tax service business, barbers shop, fast food joints etc. Also, keep in mind that minority owned businesses love to support young teens.

This hustle is about honesty. Pass out as many flyers as you can, **and do not throw any away**.

Find a moms and pops business. Be sure to have on walking shoes. Have a flyer with your name on it, along with your phone number. Walk in and ask for the owner or manager and tell them you are willing to pass out flyers. Tell the owner your desire is to see the business grow with many people.

If they say the moment is not a good time, leave them your flyer. Let them know you are ready to help when they need more business and always say Thank you for their time.

HUSTLE #6

Sign Holder

Requirements: Water and Comfortable Shoes

This hustle is similar to #5. Instead of walking and giving flyers, you stand with a large sign or poster. Use the same strategy as Hustle #5 for getting work. Tell them that you are a sign holder, and that you can hold up their sign at any corner they prefer. Always, be sure to remain in a safe place with parent's permission.

HUSTLE #7 & #8

Pet Sitting or Pet Walking

Requirements: None

Many of us know family or neighbors that have dogs, and usually don't walk them. These are good customers to start with. Put the word out that you are able to pet sit and dog walk. It is much safer to pet sit at your home than someone else's, but ask your parent if it is ok. If the dog is large put them in the back yard.

HUSTLE #9

Tutoring Service

Requirements: Knowledge of subject

Today, many parents do not have much time to tutor or help their kids with their homework. This is an opportunity for you to step in. If you are really good in subjects like English, Math, Spanish, etc., then you can offer a tutor service. You can start online and put an ad on OfferUp, Craigslist, or social media like Instagram. You can also advertise door to door by leaving a flyer on the door. Make sure to put the grade and subject you teach. Research and ask others how much you should charge.

HUSTLE #10

Trash Bin Take Out Service

Requirements: Gloves

Clients may consist of people like seniors, single mothers, or busy working people who do not have time or the ability to take out their trash.

Always start with your close neighbors, then work your way on the block. You are more familiar with those next to you. Make a flyer that states your trash bin takeout service along with your name and number. Be careful to plan your day accordingly because you can't miss putting their trash bin out before they are picked up. Don't charge too much. $20 a month service for weekly service is reasonable. Think about it… If you get 25 customers, that's $500 a month for one-day service once a week. Easy.

HUSTLE #11

Store Runner

Requirements: Energy

When I was young, I would run to the store or hamburger stand for people all day. My bike was my transportation. I remember my neighbor Butch; he was bed ridden, he was not fit to go to the store. Elderly people on my block and mothers who could not leave their children at home by themselves needed someone to run to the store for their necessities. This service isn't laborious. Like always, get your flyer that has your store runner service and phone number. When you go door to door to get business, tell them you're starting a business as a store runner and you are able to go anywhere locally. When they give you money, never spend the change on yourself. Always give them the receipts with the change. To be more convenient, add a basket to your bike.

HUSTLE #12

Talent Based On Skills

Requirements: Your skills

Talents such as playing instruments, sports, or even singing are beneficial to you in many ways. For instance, you can give lessons. You don't have to be a professional. Record yourself doing your talent. When you advertise, put the link on your flyer or cards. You can also put ad on social media.

HUSTLE #13

Mobile Barber For Kids

Please note: If you don't already know how to cut hair with clippers, please ask someone to show you or watch YouTube tutorials.

Requirement: clippers

You don't need to be a licensed barber for this hustle. Read carefully. Get yourself some clippers and a comb and/or brush. Practice cutting your own hair before trying on someone else. When I was 14, I started trying to cut my own hair. Then I started cutting my father's hair. It was nothing fancy, just a low cut. Potential customers can be in apartment buildings or the projects. Most parents can't afford a professional barber. This is why some kid's do not look kept up. You can charge $10 for a simple cut. Tell them that you don't do fancy cuts, just one style. As you do more cuts and have more experience, you will improve. Believe me. After 3 months of cutting, your phone will be ringing constantly. This will also provide you with the money to go to barbering school for your license to further yourself in the business, where you can start your own mobile barbering business or open a barber shop. I was a barber at one point.

HUSTLE #14

Mobile Hair Braider.

Requirements: Time

There are so many girls I know that do hair. If you don't know how to braid, ask someone to teach you. Or, look on YouTube. Practice on your family and friends, or even on a doll head. You don't have to do anything over the top. Just start with the basics. Also, you can do an un-braiding hair service. Once you have more experience and phots of your work, begin advertising on social media.

These last 7 hustles need a small amount of investment money to start. But, you can make much more profit. These are my favorites. You can always get paid from these instantly.

HUSTLE #15

Fresh Cookies Sales

Requirements: Oven, cookie dough, clear wrap or baggies

Everyone loves fresh baked cookies. Go to a store that sells bulk items like Sam's Club or Smart & Final. When you buy in items in bulk, you save on money. Start with chocolate chip and oatmeal cookies; these sell the most. The goal is to make the cookie large. People love big cookies. Make about 10 of each flavor, making a total of 20 cookies. There are so many places where you can start selling. Find a large shopping center to start with. Work in the parking lots. Go to stores or businesses like strip malls, nail shops, barber shops, train stations, etc. that will allow you to sell in front of their location as long as you are professional and well with customers. Selling price you should aim for $3 for one or 2 for $5. If they say not today, kindly ask for a donation.

HUSTLE #16

Fresh Brownies

Requirements: Oven, mix, clear wrap

People love fresh baked brownies. Go to a store that sells bulk items like Sam's Club or Smart and Final. Our you can make from scratch. It is important that the brownies are a good size and taste good. Start with a total of 20. Make 10 without nuts and 10 with nuts. There are so many places you can start selling. Find a large shopping center to start with. Work the parking lot or in front of businesses or stores as long as it is allowed. Prices to aim for are $3 for 1 or 2 for $5. If they say not today, ask for a donation.

HUSTLE #17

Cake Slices

Requirements: Oven, cake mix, clear wrap

People love freshly baked cakes. If you know someone who can make cakes well, ask them to teach you. You can also use cake mix if you prefer that. Begin with basic flavors like chocolate and vanilla cake. Once you build up your customer base, ask them what's their favorite flavor. Use the same strategy previously outlined to sell the cakes. Charge about $3 per cake; I do not recommend 2 for $5. Test the market and see what works best.

HUSTLE #18

World's Finest Candy Bars

Requirements: Small investment

Some people just go to the 99 Cent store and buy products then resell it for $2 or $3 per item. From my experience you should use World's Finest Chocolate candy. This is good candy with a great reputation. Google the name and order and you're set. You can earn good money selling these candies. My favorite is chocolate almond! Sell these everywhere, same spots that I put in **Hustle # 15**.

HUSTLE #19

Water & Sodas

Requirement: Ice Cooler with wheels

You can make a good deal of money selling these items, especially in the hot months. You can buy a case of water of 30 for about $4-$5. You can buy sodas and other drinks as well. Buy a bag of ice to put in your cooler. These drinks can be sold at $1 each. Go to your local train station or bus stop, or even a concert being held. There are usually many people here who need a quick drink. Hold one bottle in your hand and shout "Cold water!". When they come up to you, let them know of the other drinks you have available.

HUSTLE #20

Incense & Car Air Freshener

Requirements: Small investments

People who smoke really love these items. I sold plenty of them in my time on Crenshaw. Google "Little Trees 64 piece". These sell quick for $1. You can find an incense wholesaler in your area. Start looking in the African district, ask around and google it. Once you find a shop, they will tell you how to make them, it's really easy. I learned how to make incense at 11 years old in 10 mins. Most incense sell for $1 a pack. Combined this with car freshners and you can make easy $50 -$100 a day if you work hard. This hustle you can ask for a donation as well.

HUSTLE #21

Cut Grass

Requirement: Lawn mower, rake, bags

This is the oldest hustle in the play book. Many kids I knew cut grass to make money for school. I always loved cutting grass for pay. If you do not already own a lawn mower, purchase an affordable one or ask to borrow one from a family member if the client doesn't already have one. Start with the neighbors who you can visibly see that need their grass cut. Go to their door and tell them you're cutting front lawns and backyards for a small fee. Once they see your lawn mower, they will know you mean business. If they are not ready that day, try to set up another time with them at that moment. When you do cut grass, sweep the excess and put it in a trash bag. You can charge $15. Because every yard is different in size, I think that you should start with a donation to see what you get.

"Some encouragement to think about"

I remember when some of my friends from high school would laugh at me when they saw me selling on Crenshaw. They were spoiled, and fortunate enough to not have to work for anything. They were laughing, but in the end of the week I had a couple of hundreds in my pocket. Funny how life turned out.

Learning how to hustle at a young age resulted in me becoming entrepreneur. I opened 9 restaurants and became a consultant in the 2 largest fast food chicken chains in Los Angeles. The same guys that laughed at me when we were young came to my restaurants and put in applications to work for me-- cleaning dishes and washing the floors.

Believe in God. Stay focused. Work hard. Believe in yourself. Visualize how you want your life to be, and pursue it.

ABOUT THE AUTHOR

Phillip Johnson is a husband and father to four children. He lives in sunny Southern California. He is an entrepreneur at heart. He has owned several businesses including 9 restaurants, a trucking business, a mobile truck washing business, a kettle corn machine company and just starting Phil Lewis publishing LLC. First book "21 Hustles And Business For The Youth" Many more books to come. And Many other small Hustles that's not listed. Phil thrives on being diverse and versatile in business.

Now that you guys know my story, here are some motivational pictures to inspire you. These are some of different businesses I have owned:

Phil Lewis

The Johnson Family Building A Entrepreneurial Empire In Carson

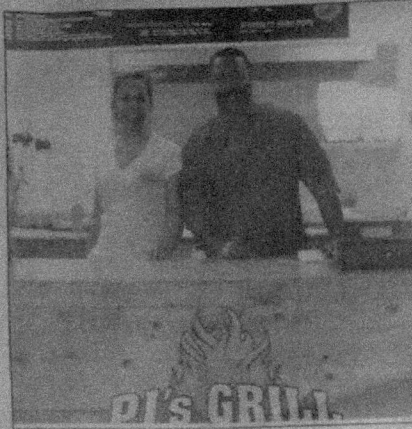

Phil & Jessika Johnsons are building a business empire in the City of Carson.

Along with their 4 amazing children, Otis, Philana, Prince & Julian, are the faces behind "PJ's Grill" a very popular resturant with the locals.

They have been in the restaurant business for 12 years.

Along with "PJ's" the Johnson's other endeavors, include Kettle Corn Equipment Manufacturing (Kettle 4 Less) and Johnson's Christmas Trees located at the Southbay Pavilion and Albertson's on Carson Street and Sepulveda.

Phil & Jessika take on the retail business wholeheartedly. They both enjoy serving people and satisfying a big appetite.

A veteran of the fast food industry, Phil's past experience includes Lewis Grilled Philly Steaks, Golden Bird Chicken and Louisiana Famous Fried Chicken, co-branding with Star Waffle and Big And Juicy Burgers.

An innovator, Phil brought many fresh ideas to the major food chains and they have carried them on as the ideas became successful.

Not to rest on their laurels of success, Phil & Jessika are stepping out on faith and creating a menu for all taste buds, including vegetarian.

Their children, Otis, Philana, Prince & Julian are also sharing in the creating of this delicious business.

Along with that menu, the Johnsons have created a great atmosphere for all ages, young and old alike. Great food, great customer service and a great atmosphere.

Come and enjoy!

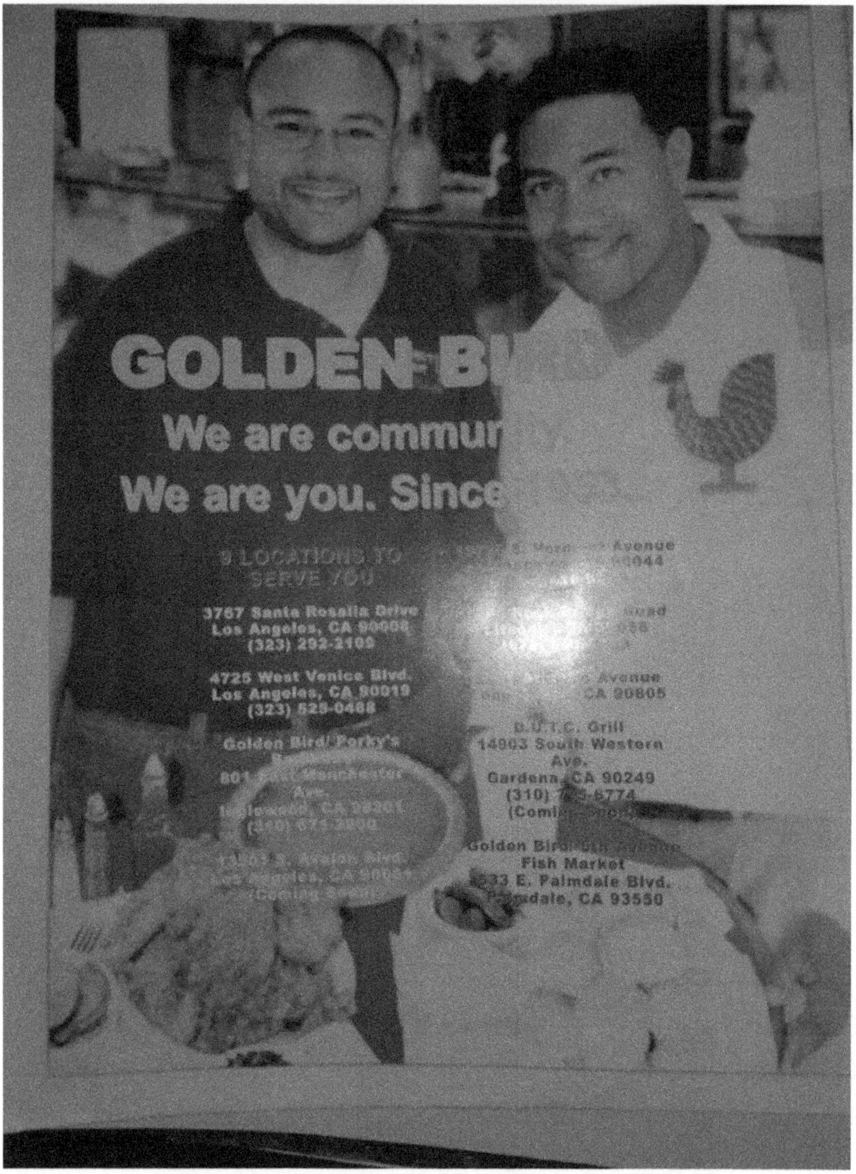

Aquil Saafir
Great food locally owned ! PJ's Grill in Carson
How far can we reach share this or your favorite black
owned business ? — with **Jessika Johnson.**

JUL 20, 2016

Since I've owned several trucks I had an idea to start a mobile truck wash business.

Hustle mentality, Entrepreneur drive

I was a consultant of the Louisiana Fried Chicken food chain. I brought in 38 new stores into the food chain. I owned and operated 8 of them. *Hustle mentality, Entrepreneur drive* I'm showing you this picture because people said me being a black man, Chinese people would not buy from me. Sold 15 license agreements to Asians @ $18,000 per store. Go figure.

Selling at a young age taught me be fearless! Yea, selling incense, candy, etc made me.

When I was a kid I would go hustle so I can afford a 3 piece combo (aka 3 piecer) from Golden Bird Chicken. I never thought I would own 3 in my early 30's…

I'm just trying to motivate you. Only thing I had was a hustle mentality, entrepreneur drive, no college degree, just hard work.

This store is the 3rd store my wife and I owned at age 28. It was located inside of a huge mall. It's special to me because people said it would not work and it did. My friends said white people don't eat chicken enough to support the business. The first 10 customers were white. Lol

PJ's owner Phil (right) and staff
over 4 years ago

PJ's Burger Crew! Most of them at least.
over 5 years ago

This store means the most to me because I started with $18,000. When I opened it was just me and my wife working and no customers. People said I would fail because the burgers weren't selling. The store only made $100 a day to start. But I kept pushing, didn't give up, after 2 weeks it was doing $1900 a day, 16 employees. A Hustle mentality, Entrepreneur drive starts at a young age.

Phil Lewis

Deanna King
— with **Jessika Johnson** and **Deanna King** at **PJ's Grill -
Homestyle Burgers, Dogs & Vegetarian.**

APR 9, 2015

Kettle corn equipment company I owned. I purchase a 16 passenger van. Hired 15 kids from Compton and Watts high schools. They went door to door selling kettle corn also we had contracts to sell in front of stores.. The kettle corn was so additive the kids named it kettle crack..Lol

Car hauling company I own, J & P Holdings LLC.

Final thoughts: Never give up on your dreams! It's true, I took losses before, but I kept going and I'm still going. I never sold drugs or rob people, I just hustled my butt off the legal way. Some of you will only hustle until you get a job and that's cool too. Just survive, don't do anything stupid to get money. You have 21 options and I'm working on the follow up book that will give you more game where you can make more money.

Alot of hustles I left out because I don't teach or practice anymore.

Here's one..

I had 5 Christmas tree lots at huge malls. I imported my trees from Oregon by the truck load. But I'm out of the game.

Stay true to you, trust in God, have faith, work hard and you will make it.

If you take a loss get back up and go again…Alright I'm done. Peace.

Phil Lewis